D0651810

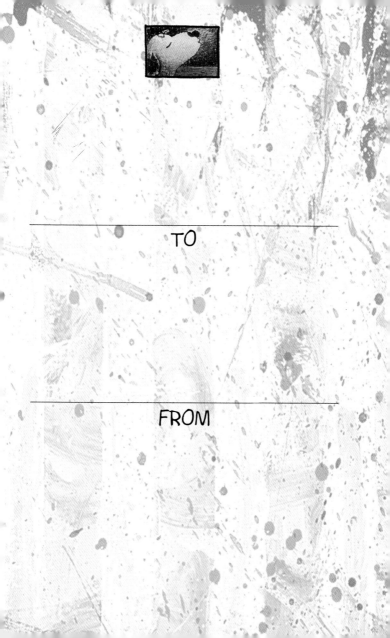

TO

FROM

MORE THAN
PUPPY LOVE

EXPRESSIONS OF AFFECTION

THEN WE

SAT ON THE EDGE OF
THE EARTH, WITH OUR
FEET DANGLING OVER THE
SIDE, AND MARVELLED
THAT WE HAD FOUND
EACH OTHER.

Erik Dillard

AS LONG

AS I HAVE YOU
THERE IS
JUST ONE
OTHER
THING
I'LL
ALWAYS
NEED—
TREMENDOUS
SELF-CONTROL.

Ashleigh Brilliant

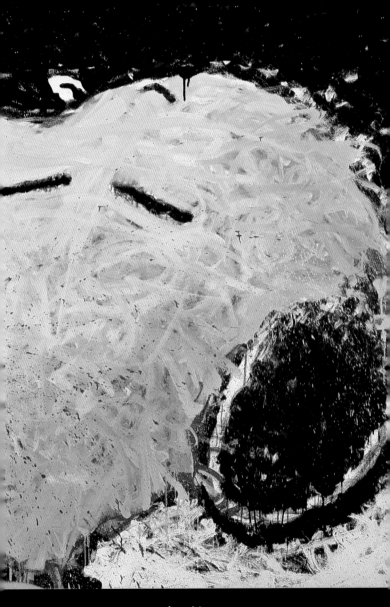

Dog Lips

IT WAS SO VERY GOOD
OF GOD TO LET MY
DREAMS COME TRUE, TO
NOTE A YOUNG GIRL'S
CHERISHED HOPES THEN
LEAD HER RIGHT TO YOU.

Ruth Bell Graham

LOVING HEARTS ARE
HAPPY HEARTS.

IF YOU LOVE SOMEONE,
THEN HURRY UP AND
SHOW IT.

Rose Zadra, age 6

AS A RESULT OF A
KISS, THERE ARISES...A
WONDERFUL FEELING
OF DELIGHT.

Ailred of Rievaulx

LOVE KNOWS NO LIMIT TO
ITS ENDURANCE, NO END
TO ITS TRUST, NO FADING
OF ITS HOPE; IT CAN
OUTLAST ANYTHING.

The First Book of Corinthians

LOVE IS, ABOVE ALL, THE
GIFT OF ONESELF.

Jean Anouilh

THE LOVE WE GIVE AWAY
IS THE ONLY LOVE WE
KEEP.

Elbert Hubbard

LOVE IS A HAPPY FEELING
THAT STAYS INSIDE YOUR
HEART FOR THE REST OF
YOUR LIFE.

Joan Walsh Anglund

EXPRESSED AFFECTION
IS...WHEN YOU WANT TO
LIGHT A GLOW IN
SOMEONE'S HEART AND TO
FEEL IT IN YOUR OWN.

Ruth Stafford Peale

IT IS NEVER TOO LATE
TO FALL IN LOVE.

TO LOVE A PERSON IS TO
LEARN THE SONG THAT IS
IN THEIR HEART, AND TO
SING IT TO THEM WHEN
THEY HAVE FORGOTTEN.

To Every Dog There Is A Season: Fall

YOU

CAN'T BLAME
GRAVITY FOR
FALLING IN LOVE.

Albert Einstein

I SEEM TO HAVE ONLY
BLACK-AND-WHITE
MEMORIES BEFORE YOU.
BUT WHEN YOU CAME
YOU BROUGHT LAUGHTER,
RED BALLOONS, SILLY
SURPRISES, FIZZ AND JOY
INTO MY LIFE.

Judith C. Grant

THERE IS NO SURPRISE
MORE MAGICAL THAN THE
SURPRISE OF BEING
LOVED. IT IS THE FINGER
OF GOD ON OUR
SHOULDER.

Charles Morgan

THERE IS NO REMEDY
FOR LOVE BUT TO LOVE
MORE.

Henry David Thoreau

PEOPLE WHO THROW
KISSES ARE HOPELESSLY
LAZY.

Bob Hope

LOVE. NO GREATER THEME
CAN BE EMPHASIZED. NO
STRONGER MESSAGE CAN
BE PROCLAIMED. NO FINER
SONG CAN BE SUNG.

Charles R. Swindoll

THOUGH IT RAINS,
I WON'T GET WET:
I'LL USE YOUR LOVE
FOR AN UMBRELLA.

Japanese Folk Song

THE GREATEST GIFT IS
A PORTION OF YOURSELF.

MANY WATERS CANNOT
QUENCH LOVE; RIVERS
CANNOT WASH IT AWAY.

Song of Solomon

OUR LOVE IS LIKE THE
MISTY RAIN THAT FALLS
SOFTLY—BUT FLOODS
THE RIVER.

African Proverb

LOVE IS THE SEED OF
ALL HOPE. IT IS THE
ENTICEMENT TO TRUST,
TO RISK, TO TRY,
TO GO ON.

Gloria Gaither

THE HEART HAS ITS
REASONS THAT REASON
KNOWS NOTHING OF.

Blaise Pascal

Big, Loud Screaming Blonde

WHERE'S
THE KABOOM?
THERE WAS SUPPOSED BE
AN EARTH-SHATTERING
KABOOM!

Marvin the Martian

WHEN YOU LOVE SOMEONE,
SIT CLOSE BY AND
NUZZLE THEM GENTLY.

BLESSED IS THE
INFLUENCE OF ONE
TRUE, LOVING HUMAN
SOUL ON ANOTHER.

George Eliot

LOVE IS WHAT YOU'VE
BEEN THROUGH WITH
SOMEBODY.

James Thurber

TO GET THE FULL VALUE
OF JOY YOU MUST HAVE
SOMEONE TO DIVIDE
IT WITH.

Mark Twain

MY LIFE HAS BEEN THE
AWAITING YOU. YOUR
FOOTFALL WAS MY OWN
HEART'S BEAT.

Paul Valery

SOMETIMES I NEED WHAT
ONLY YOU CAN PROVIDE—
YOURSELF!

TWO ARE BETTER THAN
ONE.... FOR IF THEY FALL,
ONE WILL LIFT UP
THE OTHER.

The Book of Ecclesiastes

TO LOVE AND TO BE
LOVED IS THE GREATEST
HAPPINESS OF EXISTENCE.

Syndey Smith

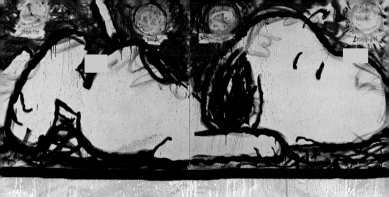

I LOVE YOU, NOT ONLY
FOR WHAT YOU ARE
BUT FOR WHAT I AM
WHEN I AM WITH YOU.

Roy Croft

LOVE IS AN IRRESISTIBLE
DESIRE TO BE
IRRESISTIBLY DESIRED.

Robert Frost

LOVE IS LIKE AN
HOURGLASS, WITH THE
HEART FILLING UP AS
THE BRAIN EMPTIES.

Jules Renard

Sticky, Wet, Romantic Kiss On the Love Boat

THE KISS—

SOMETHING MADE
OF NOTHING, TASTING
VERY SWEET.

M. E. Buell

I NEVER THOUGHT I
COULD LOVE ANYTHING
WITHOUT FOUR WHEELS
AND A STICK SHIFT.

Michael McFarlane

LOVE TAKES RISKS.

Janette Oke

ANY TIME THAT IS
NOT SPENT ON LOVE
IS WASTED.

Tasso

LOVE IS THE ONLY GAME
THAT IS NOT CALLED ON
ACCOUNT OF DARKNESS.

KISS RHYMES WITH
BLISS IN FACT, AS
WELL AS VERSE.

Lord Byron

THE LANGUAGE OF
LOVERS IS THE LANGUAGE
OF WASTE. THEY ARE
GLAD TO WASTE TIME
WITH EACH OTHER, FOR
THEY ARE PLEASED WITH
THE COMPANY.

LOVE IS THAT CONDITION
IN WHICH THE HAPPINESS
OF ANOTHER PERSON IS
ESSENTIAL TO YOUR OWN.

Robert Heinlein

LOVE WILL HAVE THE
WHOLE AND NOT A PART.

Longfellow

IF YOU GET A HUG
ENJOY IT. AND WHEN YOU
LEAVE FOR THE DAY,
ALWAYS TAKE YOUR HUG
WITH YOU!

Barbara Johnson

LOVE AND A COUGH
CANNOT BE HID.

George Herbert

LOVE IN THE HEART
WASN'T PUT THERE TO
STAY; LOVE ISN'T LOVE
'TIL YOU GIVE IT AWAY.

Oscar Hammerstein II

Bird Lips in a Blonde Bombshell Wig

LOVE

IS A GREAT
BEAUTIFIER.

Louisa May Alcott

LOVE IS THE GREATEST
REFRESHMENT IN LIFE.

Pablo Picasso

LOVE IS WHAT MAKES
TWO PEOPLE SIT IN THE
MIDDLE OF A BENCH
WHEN THERE'S PLENTY
OF ROOM AT BOTH ENDS.

AT THE TOUCH OF LOVE,
EVERYONE BECOMES
A POET.

Plato

A KISS IS A SECRET TOLD
TO THE MOUTH INSTEAD
OF TO THE EAR.

Edmond Rostand

LOVE IS THE STRANGE
BEWILDERMENT WHICH
OVERTAKES ONE PERSON
ON ACCOUNT OF ANOTHER
PERSON.

James Thurber

WHAT THE WORLD REALLY
NEEDS IS MORE LOVE AND
LESS PAPER WORK.

Pearl Bailey

IF THERE IS ANYTHING
BETTER THAN TO BE
LOVED, IT IS LOVING.

LIFE IS A FLOWER
OF WHICH LOVE IS
THE HONEY.

Victor Hugo

LOVE IS EVERYTHING.
IT IS THE KEY OF LIFE,
AND ITS INFLUENCES
ARE THOSE THAT MOVE
THE WORLD.

Ralph Waldo Emerson

ALL OF US NEED MORE
LOVE THAN WE DESERVE.

THESE THREE REMAIN:
FAITH, HOPE AND LOVE.
BUT THE GREATEST OF
THESE IS LOVE.

The First Book of Corinthians

As The Sun Sets Slowly In The West, We Bid You A Fine Farewell

LOVE

DOESN'T MAKE
THE WORLD GO
ROUND. LOVE IS WHAT
MAKES THE RIDE
WORTHWHILE.

Franklin P. Jones

I WILL NEVER LOSE THE
WONDER OF YOU. I WILL
FOREVER ENJOY THE
BEAUTY OF YOU. I WILL
ALWAYS TREASURE THE
MEMORY OF YOU. YOU
ARE MY LOVE, MY GIFT!

Roy Lessin

A KISS IS LIP SERVICE
TO LOVE.

Warren Goldberg

MY HEART IS EVER AT
YOUR SERVICE.

Shakespeare

TO FEEL LOVE GIVES
PLEASURE TO ONE; TO
EXPRESS IT GIVES
PLEASURE TO TWO.

Janette Oke

NOT WHERE I BREATHE,
BUT WHERE I LOVE,
I LIVE.

Robert Southey

THE SIGHT OF YOU...IS
AS NECESSARY FOR ME
AS IS THE SUN FOR
THE SPRING FLOWERS.

Marguerite of Valois

DON'T EVER FORGET THAT
I WILL ALWAYS LOVE YOU!

MY LOVE IS MINE AND
I AM HIS.

Song of Solomon

LOVE IS REACHING,
TOUCHING AND CARING,
SHARING SUNSHINE AND
FLOWERS, SO MANY HAPPY
HOURS TOGETHER.

KISSES KEPT ARE WASTED;
LOVE IS TO BE TASTED.

E. V. Cooke

I WILL PART WITH
ANYTHING FOR YOU
BUT YOU.

Lady Mary Wortley Montague

THOU HAST

NO FAULTS,
OR I NO
FAULTS
CAN SPY;
THOU
ART ALL
BEAUTY,
OR ALL
BLINDNESS I.

C. Cadrington

Don't Look Now

MATH IS LIKE LOVE—
A SIMPLE IDEA BUT IT
CAN GET COMPLICATED.

ONE DOES NOT FALL "IN"
OR "OUT" OF LOVE. ONE
GROWS IN LOVE.

Leo Buscaglia

LAUGHING AT OURSELVES
AS WELL AS WITH EACH
OTHER GIVES A
SURPRISING SENSE
OF TOGETHERNESS.

Hazel C. Lee

LAUGHTER IS A NOISY
SMILE!

Steven Goldberg

I WISH I COULD TELL
YOU THE DAY, THE HOUR,
THE MINUTE MY LOVE
FOR YOU BECAME REAL.
I ONLY KNOW IT SEEMS
I'VE LOVED YOU FOREVER.

TO LOVE IS TO RECEIVE
A GLIMPSE OF HEAVEN.

Karen Sunde

WHAT WE LOVE WE SHALL
GROW TO RESEMBLE.

St. Bernard of Clairvaux

KISSING IS A MEANS OF GETTING TWO PEOPLE SO CLOSE TOGETHER THAT THEY CAN'T SEE ANYTHING WRONG WITH EACH OTHER.

G. Yasenak

NO LOVE GIVEN AWAY IS EVER WASTED!

Gloria Gaither

AN ANNIVERSARY SAYS,
"THINK OF THE
DREAMS YOU HAVE
WEATHERED TOGETHER.
THEY ARE INTIMATE
ACCOMPLISHMENTS."

Charles R. Swindoll

REAL LOVE STORIES NEVER
HAVE ENDINGS.

Richard Bach

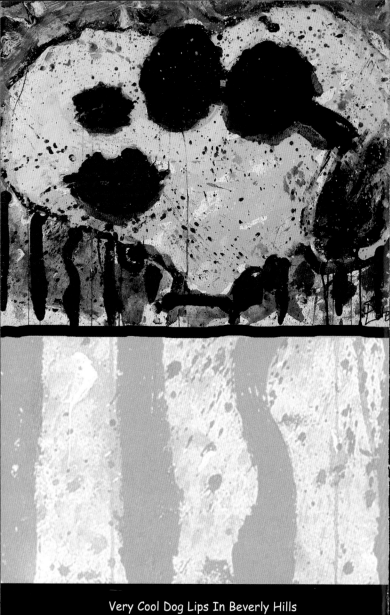

Very Cool Dog Lips In Beverly Hills

I LOVE

YOU, FOR THE
PART OF ME THAT
YOU BRING OUT.

Roy Croft

MORE THAN PUPPY LOVE
EXPRESSIONS OF AFFECTION

Bright, expressive paintings by Tom Everhart,
the only artist authorized by Charles Schulz
to illustrate Peanuts characters, are paired with
lighthearted, fun-loving sentiments in this
celebration of love.

Artwork copyright © 1999 UFS
Design by Lecy Design
Text copyright © 1999 FrontPorch Books,
a division of Garborg's, LLC

Published by Garborg's, LLC
P. O. Box 20132, Bloomington, MN 55420

ISBN 1-58375-465-2
Printed in Mexico